I0467321

Design & Concepts L.L.C
August Issue 2014

House of
Lisabeth Design
Magazine

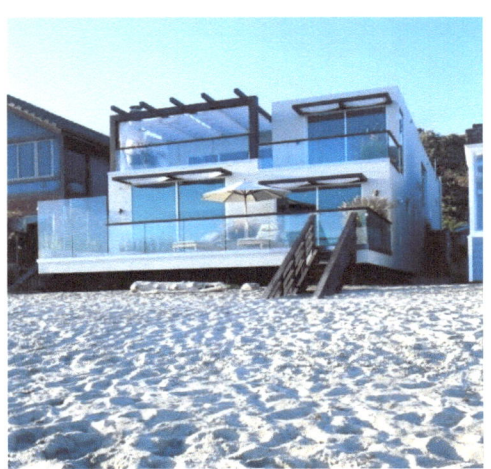

Today's Issue:

- *Doggy's world*
- *Fashion No's*
- *Design or Not*
- *Featured Business*

House of Lisabeth Design Magazine 2014

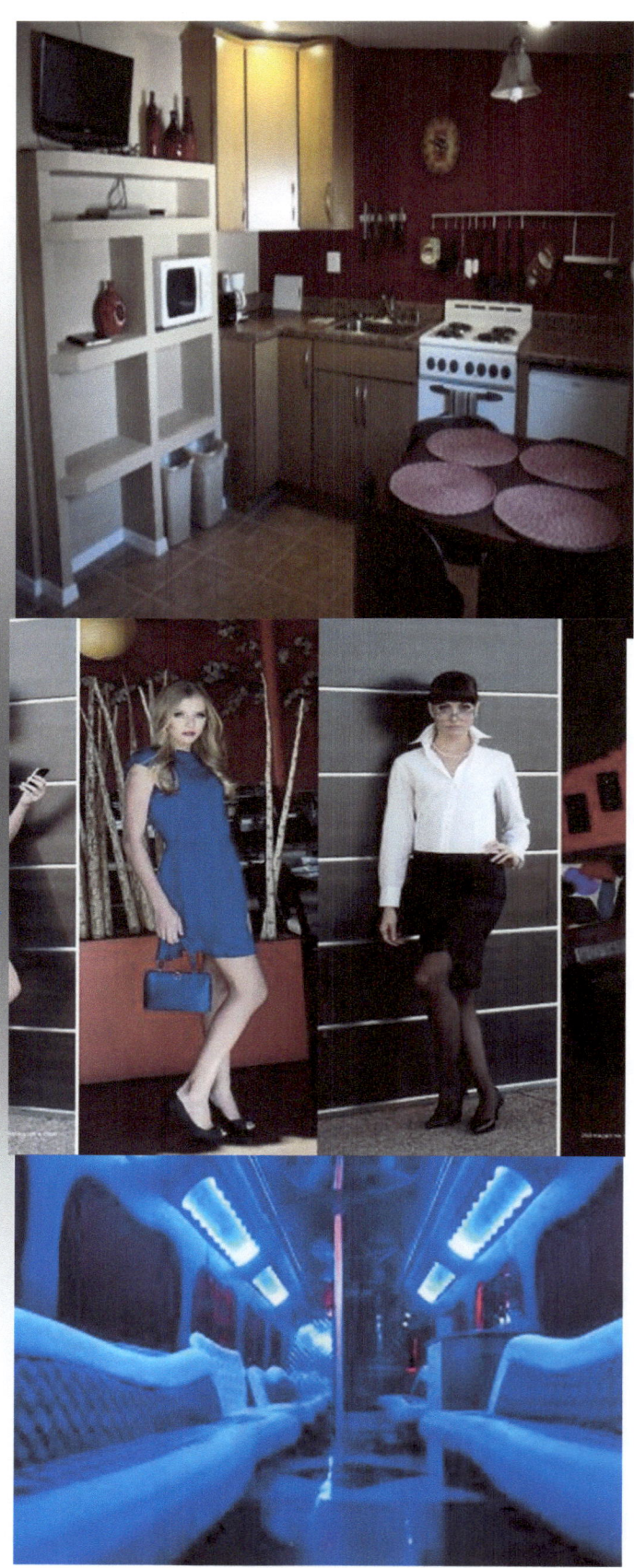

Health Trends: What We Know And What You Need To Know

Is taking your medication important to you?

Is taking medication important to you? You need to know these things when you are bombarded every day with things like aspirin to prescribed to over the counter. Your medication is the key to you living everyday health and so we went looking for ways to help better improve on the way you take your medication and some more on what you might like. Check this out……

High tech meds, is new and now part of a new type of testing. This type of testing is done for genetics purposes. Why you may ask is because matching your medication and individualizing treatment protocol is number one. With industries like this companies spend millions upon millions of dollars to get these perfected effective medication out to the public. It is our chance and our point to prove that from a stem of our DNA we can make newer drugs and older drugs more effective and direct.

Companies like 23and me, also Genomind are leveraging new technology to allow doctors to highly personalize treatment. We've been using these tests with patients and find even better treatment outcomes."
—Jeffrey A. Morrison, M.D., of the Morrison Center, which specializes in integrative medicine and nutrition.

Could this be a break through? We hope and for now we must rely on our own practices when taking prescribed medication.

Health Trends: What We Know And What You Need To Know

Is indigestion bothering you?

Indigestion is often a sign of an underlying problem, such as gastroesophageal reflux disease (GERD), ulcers, or gallbladder disease, rather than a condition of its own.
Also called dyspepsia, indigestion is a term used to describe a feeling of fullness or discomfort during or after a meal. It can be accompanied by burning or pain in the upper stomach.

Some symptoms are bloating, belly ach, gas etc. This is only a few signs but after a while if it doesn't go away then you start to realize you have a problem.

People of all ages and of both sexes are affected by indigestion. It's extremely common. An individual's risk increases with excess alcohol consumption, use of drugs that may irritate the stomach (such as aspirin), other conditions where there is an abnormality in the digestive tract such as an ulcer and emotional problems such as anxiety or depression.

Some of the few items to remember is that when it comes to indigestion 2 main things can be the root of it. One is Lifestyle. They say you are what you eat and so by being aware of that statement you know that you are what you eat literally. Overall you want to remember things like eating too much or eating too fast or eating in high stress times can be a factor. Also drinking too much alcohol and smoking can be another factor. Another root of indigestion is disease. Things like stomach cancer, ulcers, infections and irritable bowel syndrome is another cause.

Editors Feature

Answers are here......

Things like this is easily treatable with the right kind of treatments. Things like aspirin and painkillers are good for swelling or even the pain itself. Also estrogen and oral contraceptive and steroid medication is also recommended for bloating and possibly more. There are other things like certain antibiotics and thyroid medication that add on but the most important thing to remember is that you want to treat it as soon as possible.

Because really who wants a cranky person around after having fried chicken right?

So have fun eat healthy and don't forget to keep in mind your health, mind and body.

August Events Around The World Coming Up!

The 33rd Annual Telluride Mushroom Festival
August 15-19 2014

National Radio Day
August 20 2014

The 57th Annual Monterey Jazz Festival
September 10-24 2014

Street Party, Phoenix Arizona Downtown
October 14 2014

3rd Annual Zombie Walk, Phoenix Arizona
October 25 2014

3 TV Phoenix 10k & Half Marathon
November 2 2014

Up-Coming Festivals in Arizona

Sedona Hummingbird Festival , August 1-3 2014
Sedona Performing Art Center
Sedona, Arizona

Sedona Hummingbird Festival – Sedona Performing Arts Center, presentations by hummingbird experts in many interest areas: science, gardening, photography, conservation and regional species studies, and tours, $17 for 1-day presentations pass; 3-day presentations pass $45; children under 12 free with a paying adult, 800-529-3699 or http://www.sedonahummingbirdfestival.com

Annual Harvest, August 3rd 2014
Sonoita, Vineyards
Elgin

Come join us for our Annual Harvest Festival
Saturday & Sunday, August 2nd and 3rd, 2014
_10:00am - 4:00pm_

66th Annual Vigilant Days, August 8-10 2014
Tombstone, Arizona

66th Annual Vigilante Days – Wild West history comes to life in the streets of Tombstone, "the town too tough to die," street entertainment, 1880s fashion show, 10K, shoot-outs, hangings, concert, chili cook-off, saloon girls, http://www.tombstonechamber.com or http://www.tombstonevigilantes.com

Old Bisbee Brewing Company's Presents The 4th Annual Pirates of the High Desert, August 8-10 2014
Bisbee Arizona

Old Bisbee Brewing Company Presents the 4th Annual Pirates of the High Desert - Old Bisbee Brewing Company, costume contest, city wide treasure hunt, burlesque show, music everywhere, art walk, exotic rum tastings, food and lots of fun, 520-432-BREW (2739) or http://www.discoverbisbee.com or https://www.facebook.com/BisbeePirates

Check out some pictures from last years festivals.....

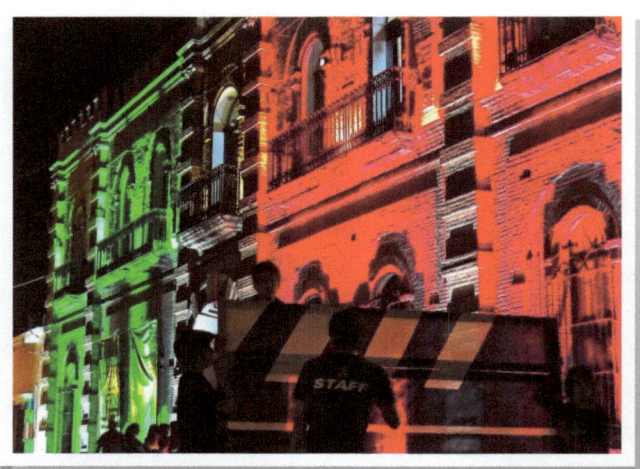

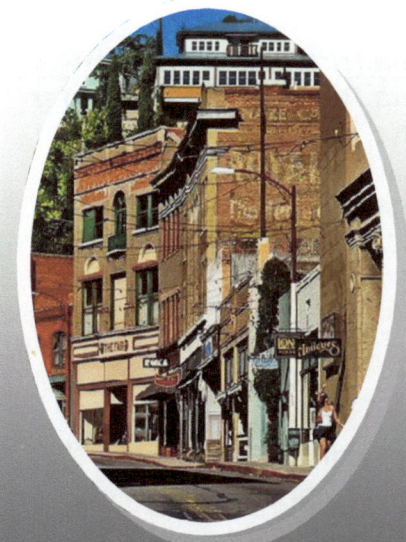

Enjoy a night out in Bisbee, Arizona

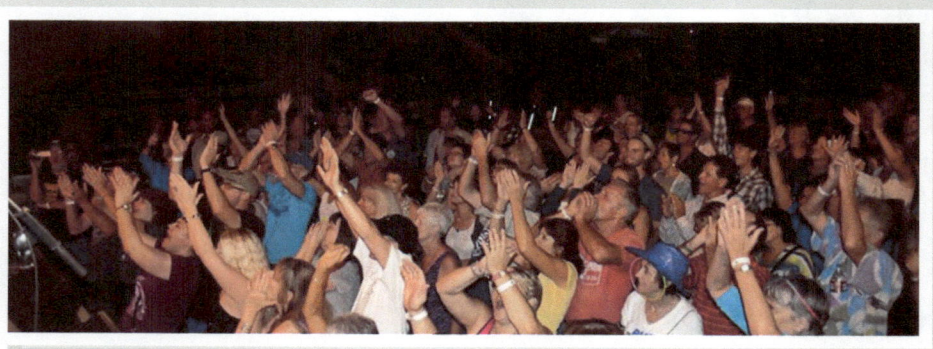

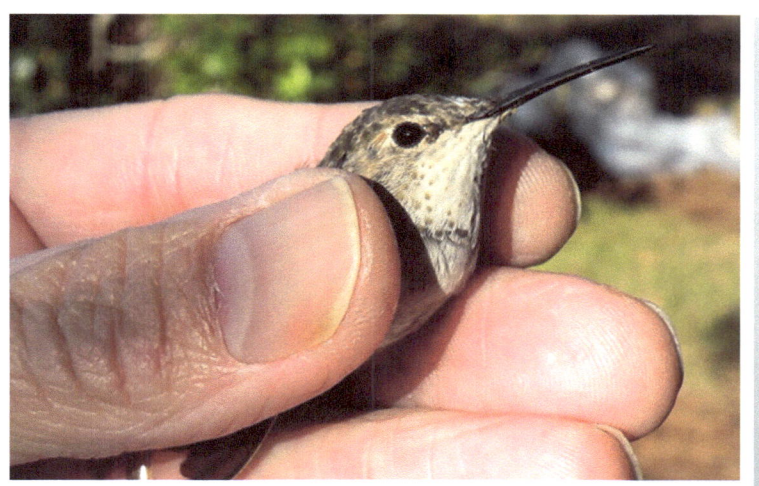

Sedona & Verde Valley Vacations
The place to plan your next vacation!

Sedona-Arizona-Vacations.com

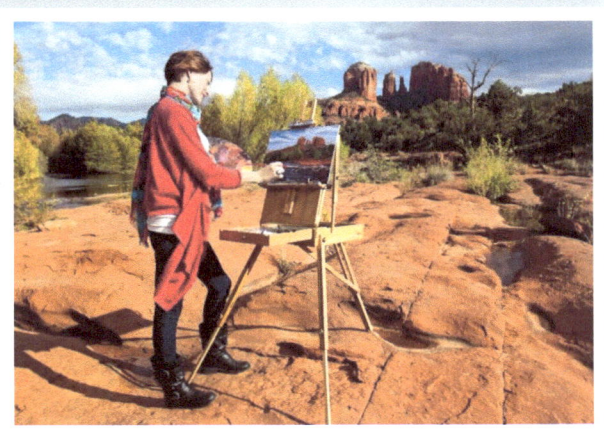

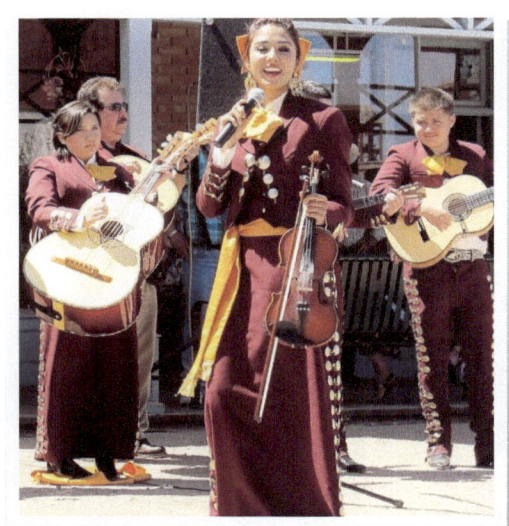

Check out Tombstone Arizona!

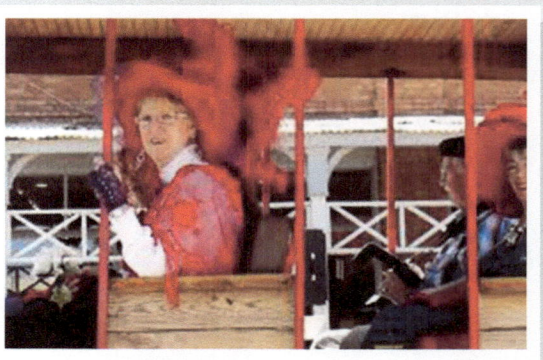

Want to place your business in our magazine? Come Advertise with us!

See back of issue for more information!

The World of Entertainment

TOP PICKS OF THIS MONTH.....

The Book of Life
By: Deborah Harkness
The highly anticipated finale to the #1 New York Times bestselling trilogy that began with A Discovery of Witches
After traveling through time in Shadow of Night, the second book in Deborah Harkness's enchanting series, historian and witch Diana Bishop and vampire scientist Matthew Clairmont return to the present to face new crises and old enemies

Tom Clancy: Support and Defend
By: Mark Greaney
One of Tom Clancy's most storied characters, Dominic Caruso, is the only one who can stop America's secrets from falling into enemy hands in this blockbuster new novel written by Clancy's longtime coauthor

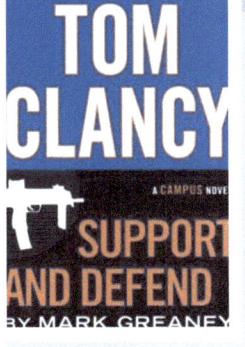

The 5 Mistakes Every Investor Makes and How to Avoid Them: Getting Investing Right
By: Peter Mallouk
offers a lively description of the common mistakes investors make in their quest to beat the market. Avoiding these pitfalls and following an informed, disciplined approach can improve the odds of a positive investment outcome."
—David G. Booth, Chairman and Co-Chief Exec-

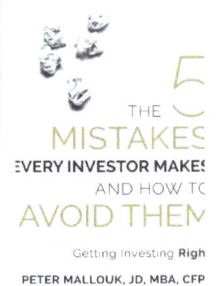

Dog Eat Dog World Presents:
Music Events, Concerts and Venues:

U.S. Airways Center Presents

Phoenix Mercury VS Atlanta Dream
August 5th at 7pm

Phoenix Mercury VS Los Angeles Sparks
August 16

WWE Smackdown
August 19

201 E Jefferson St. Phoenix, AZ 85004 602-379-7878

Marquee Theatre Presents

38 Special
August 1

311 with Dj Soulman
August 2

The Summer National Tour Featuring Offspring
August 29

730 N Mill Ave, Tempe AZ 85281, 480-829-0607

Fashion No or not....
Brought to you by: Lisabeths Design

Diamonds or Puppies

Fashion never loses its eye on diamonds. When all else fails diamonds is the way to go. Diamonds a girls best friend. It's the ever trendy thing that we know.
Diamond fashion began with the imports and exports of our hearts. The most famous dealers are Cambridge, Zales, Helzberg so on and so fourth. Diamond fashion can be as classic as the simple diamond ring cut for marriage, so on and so fourth also as fashionable as diamond and pearls mixed to a beautiful necklace or bracelet.
Diamond Fashion can be easily worn every day if you decide on the right look and the right combination. A fashionable look can be as simple as a diamond necklace or complex diamond ring necklace and bracelet. To complete the look a simple elegant black dress or a nice top and pair of jeans. Either way you are sure to make a splash.

Here are some places to shop for diamonds

1. www.bluenile.com
2. Www.helzberg.com
3. Www.zales.com
4. Www.adiamor.com

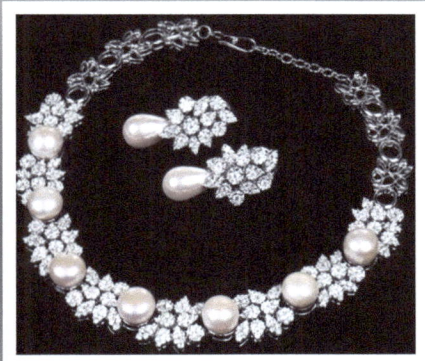

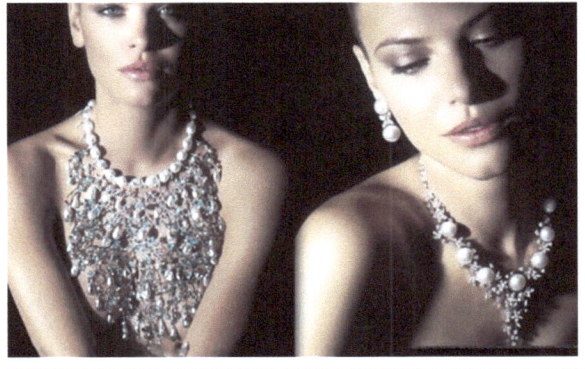

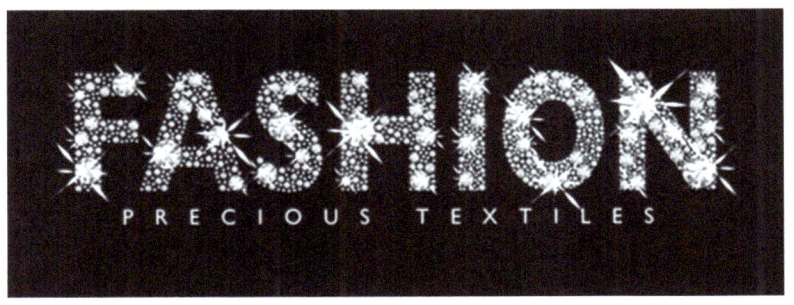

DESIGN SEO STYLE CREATE SEO LIFE

Marketing in black-and-white Vs Today's World
Design concepts is known for being at reach we pride ourselves on having all of our products technology and marketing strategies available at hand. But what about a few years ago or what about our Beginning we soon realized that we weren't the only one thinking of innovation and technology but that we came from innovation and technology that was beyond our years things that were basic.

It's those kinds of ideas of basic and simplicity that we want to continue.

Our latest addition is our Marketing Services.

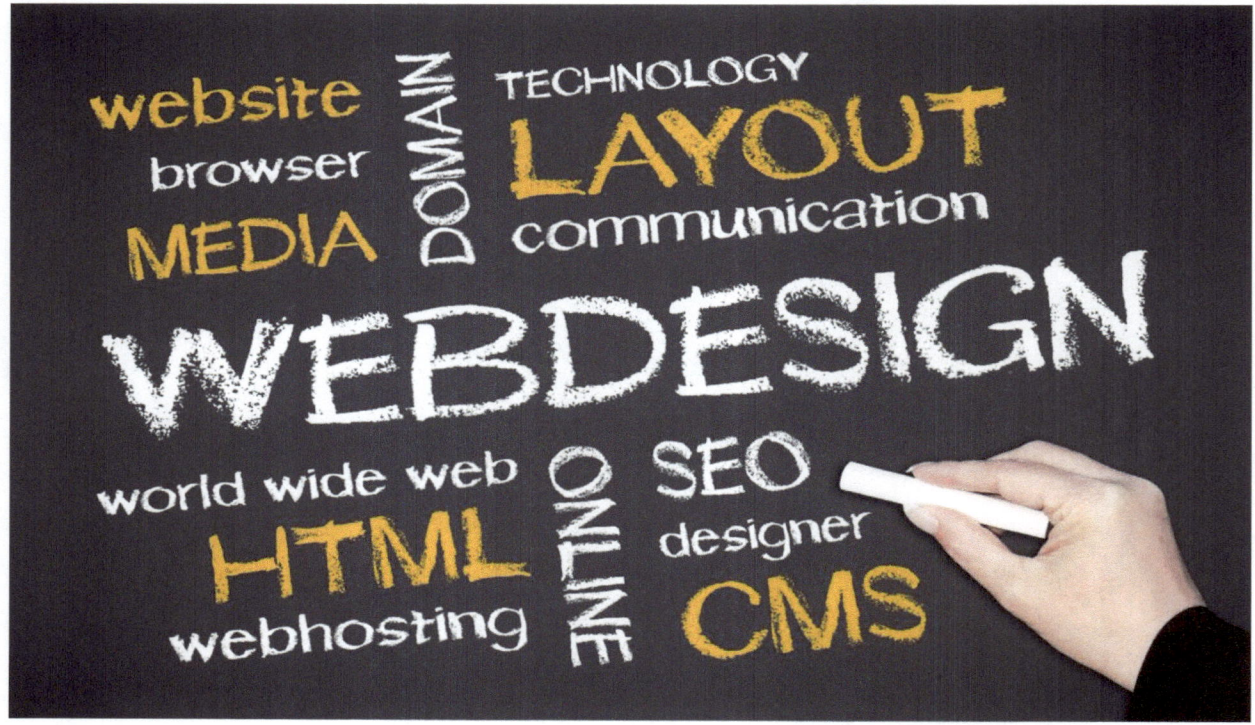

Featured Business:
Business of today tomorrow

Kamann Wana Hawaiian treats

From the customers perspectives..........

My first 5 star rating. Not enough words to describe this place. I've been looking for a shaved ice place since I moved to AZ from HAWAII. Glad I found this place. As authentic as you can get, Kevin brought all his talents from Oahu to this place. Plenty of flavors to choose from. He is nice enough to let you try samples if it's your first time. Atmosphere is as good as it gets besides actually being on north shore. Will gladly be back sooner than later.

My kids love this place. Too bad we live so far away. Sometimes we drive all across town just for a snow cone. Lucky for my kids this place is close to their pediatrician so they get a treat every time they are sick. Prices are very reasonable and they really do have the best shaved ice.

Located at:

13825 N 19th Ave Phoenix, AZ 85023

Get Directions
Phone number (602) 819-3050

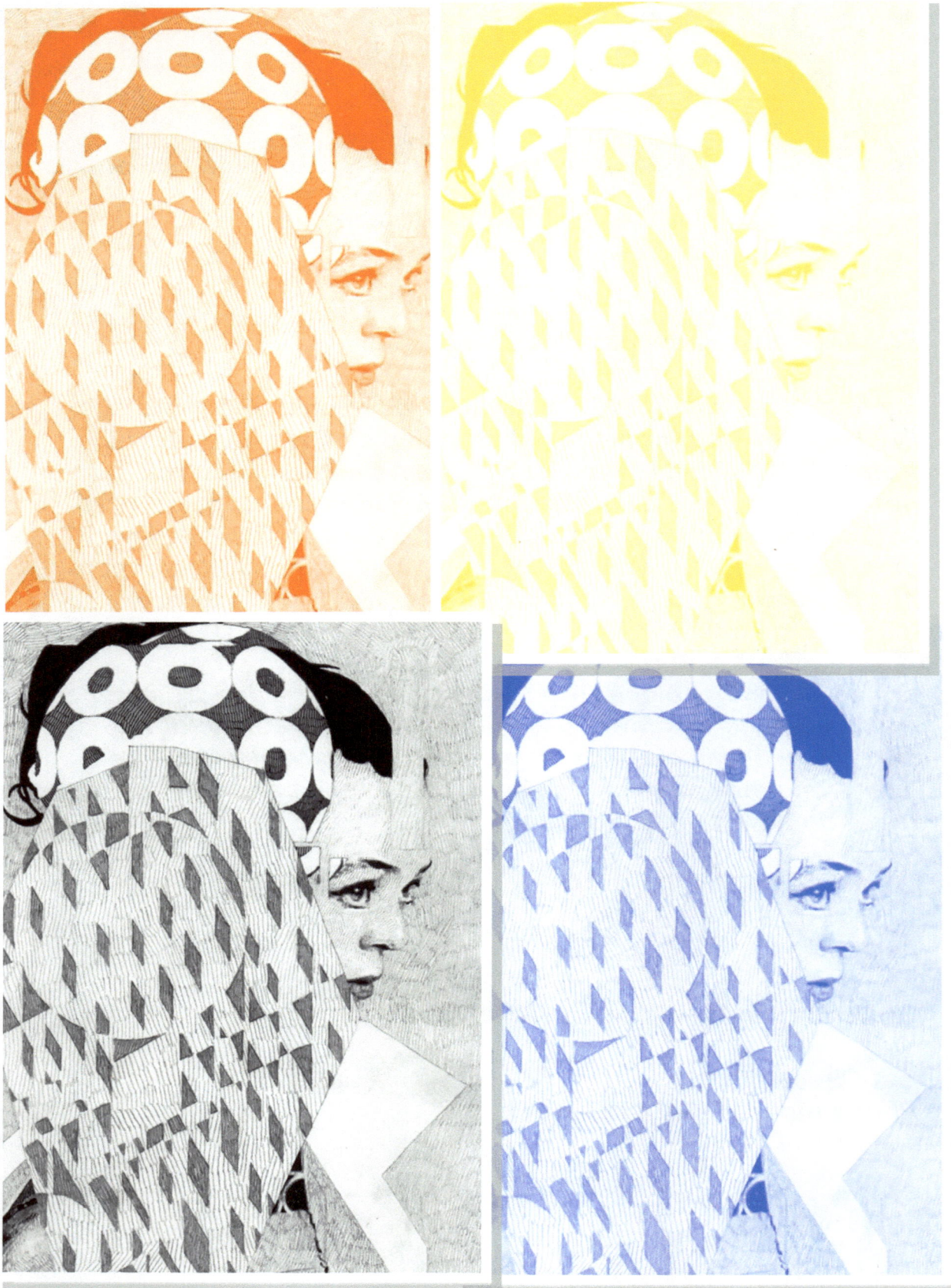

French-speaking painters continued the Mannerist conventions even later than did those at Haarlem, and at Nancy (capital of the independent duchy of Lorraine before 1633 and again from 1697 to 1766) a group of artists around Jacques Bellange and Jacques Callot was responsible for the last great flowering of the Mannerist style in Europe. By comparison, painting in Paris during the first decades of the 17th century was relatively insignificant, with the exception of that of Claude Vignon, who exchanged his Mannerist training for a style based on Elsheimer and to a lesser extent Lastman, and who in the 1620s revealed a remarkable knowledge of the earliest paintings of Rembrandt. The return of Simon Vouet to Paris, however, marked the arrival of the Baroque in France. The earliest paintings from his stay in Rome are strikingly vigorous essays in the Caravaggesque style, but by 1620 he was painting in an eclectic, classicizing style based on the early Baroque painters active there, including Giovanni Lanfranco and Guido Reni. This style he brought back to France, enjoying until his death an immense success in Paris as a decorator and painter of large-scale altarpieces; even the return of Nicolas Poussin failed to shake his position. Poussin's activity in Paris is of relatively little importance compared with the remainder of his career in Rome, but the large number of works commissioned by French patrons then and subsequently was an important factor in the formation of the French predilection for classicism. Another Frenchman, Claude Lorrain in Rome, had his sources in the romantic landscapes of the late Mannerists. By 1640 he established an international reputation. Both Poussin and Claude had been formed in Rome, but they remained typically French with a spiritual seriousness subjugated entirely to the laws of reason.

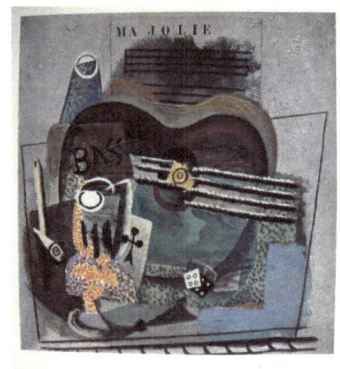 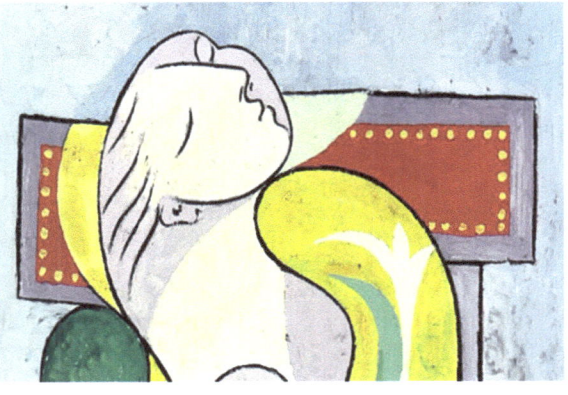 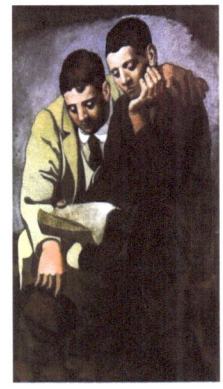

Trendy News What You Want To Know

When last we saw Olivia Pope, she was flying off into the sunset (or maybe just flying off) with Jake by her side—leaving behind a broken Fitz, who'd just lost his son and realized some horrible things about his father. D.C. now rests in the hands of Olivia's own father, who once again took over B-613. So what awaits the team when season four starts up? How about a new face?

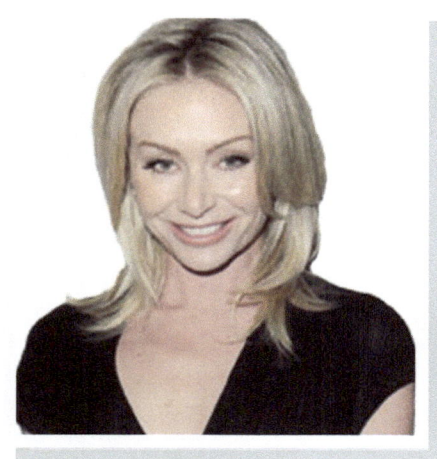

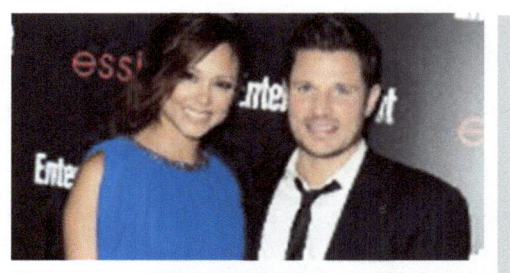

*Nick Lachey and Vanessa Minnillo having baby no. 2
Not sure why this guy is still famous but I'd rather read about him knocking up the hot wife instead of Kayne's latest racist rant......—quotes from fans,*

*This after finding out Nick Lachey and Vanessa Minnillo is having baby # 2 .
Minnillo and Lachey became engaged in November 2010,[22] and married on July 15, 2011, on Sir Richard Branson's private Necker Island in the British Virgin Islands.*

New Technology For The Modern Geek

Cubelets - Modular Robotics Construction Kit

Cubelets robotic cubes can be snapped together to make a variety of robots with no programming and no wires. You can build robots that drive around on a tabletop, respond to light and other objects, and have surprisingly lifelike behavior. But instead of programming that behavior, you snap the Cubelets together and watch the behavior emerge like a flock of birds or a swarm of bees.

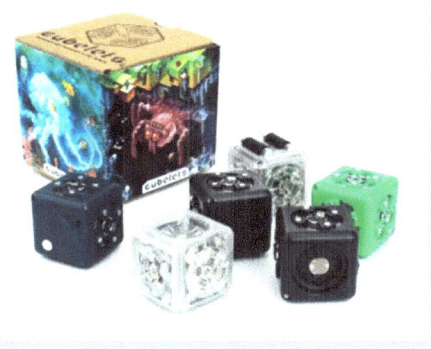

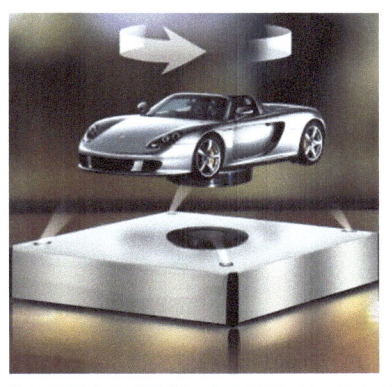

Levitron Revolution Platform With EZ Float Technology

Although Ernshaw's Theorem states that it is impossible to create a static magnetic field that can levitate an object stably on all axes, inventor Bill Hones' latest device will allow you to levitate objects weighing up to 13 ounces! The magnetic hover disc can float a small item in mid-air, while four white accent LEDs illuminate it as it continuously revolves around in space. Spotlight your models, jewelry or geology specimens, and other collectibles in the most spectacular way possible!

New Technology Vs. The other guys

Techno-progressivism maintains that accounts of "progress" should focus on scientific and technical dimensions, as well as ethical and social ones. For most techno-progressive perspectives, then, the growth of scientific knowledge or the accumulation of technological powers will not represent the achievement of proper progress unless and until it is accompanied by a just distribution of the costs, risks, and benefits of these new knowledges and capacities. At the same time, for most techno-progressive critics and advocates, the achievement of better democracy, greater fairness, less violence, and a wider rights culture are all desirable, but inadequate in themselves to confront the quandaries of contemporary technological societies unless and until they are accompanied by progress in science and technology to support and implement these values.[2]

Strong techno-progressive positions include support for the civil right of a person to either maintain or modify his or her own mind and body, on his or her own terms, through informed, consensual recourse to, or refusal of, available therapeutic or enabling biomedical technology.[3] Bioconservatism (a portmanteau word combining "biology" and "conservatism") is a stance of hesitancy about technological development especially if it is perceived to threaten a given social order. Strong bioconservative positions include opposition to genetic modification of food crops, the cloning and genetic engineering of livestock and pets, and, most prominently, rejection of the genetic, prosthetic, and cognitive modification of human beings to overcome what are broadly perceived as current human biological and cultural limitations.[1][2]

Bioconservatives range in political perspective from right-leaning religious and cultural conservatives to left-leaning environmentalists and technology critics. What unifies bioconservatives is skepticism about medical and other biotechnological transformations of the living world.[4][5][6][7] Typically less sweeping as a critique of technological society than bioluddism, the bioconservative perspective is characterized by its defense of the natural, deployed as a moral category.[1][2]

Enhancement

The Industrial Revolution was the transition to new manufacturing processes in the period from about 1760 to sometime between 1820 and 1840. This transition included going from hand production methods to machines, new chemical manufacturing and iron production processes, improved efficiency of water power, the increasing use of steam power, and the development of machine tools. It also included the change from wood and other bio-fuels to coal.

Textiles were the dominant industry of the Industrial Revolution in terms of employment, value of output and capital invested. Textiles were also the first to use modern production methods.[2]

The Industrial Revolution marks a major turning point in history; almost every aspect of daily life was influenced in some way. In particular, average income and population began to exhibit unprecedented sustained growth. Some economists, such as Robert E. Lucas, Jr., argue that the real impact of the Industrial Revolution was that "for the first time in history, the living standards of the masses of ordinary people have begun to undergo sustained growth ... Nothing remotely like this economic behavior is mentioned by the classical economists, even as a theoretical possibility."[3]

Others, however, argue that while growth of the economy's overall productive powers was unprecedented during the Industrial Revolution, living standards for the majority of the population did not grow meaningfully until the late 19th and 20th centuries, and that in many ways workers' living standards declined under early capitalism: for instance, studies have shown that real wages in Britain only increased 15% between the 1780s and 1850s, and that life expectancy in Britain did not begin to dramatically increase until the 1870s.[4][5]

The Industrial Revolution began in Great Britain and spread to Western Europe and the United States within a few decades. The precise start and end of the Industrial Revolution is debated among historians. Eric Hobsbawm held that it 'broke out' in Britain in the 1780s and was not fully felt until the 1830s or 1840s,[6] while T. S. Ashton held that it occurred roughly between 1760 and 1830.[7]

Industrial Revolution

Social apps and more
Find us !

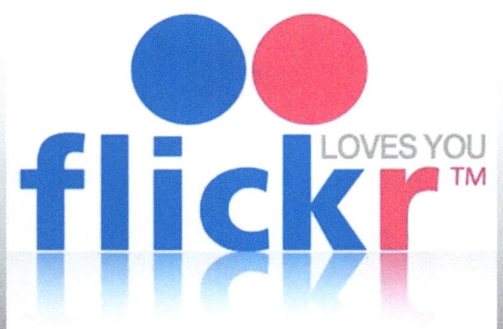

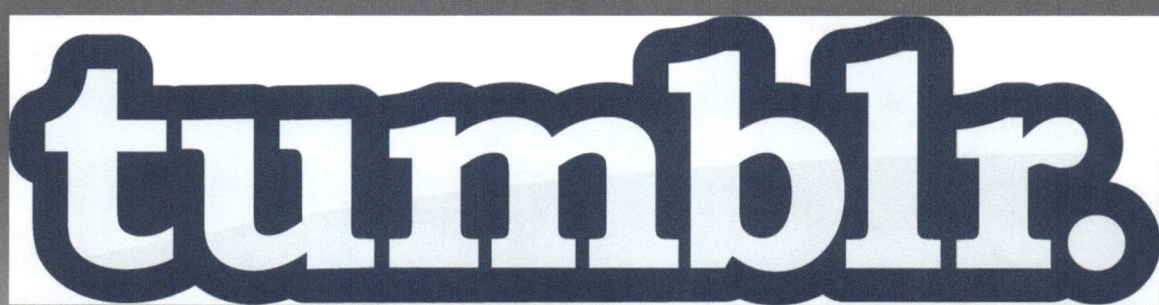

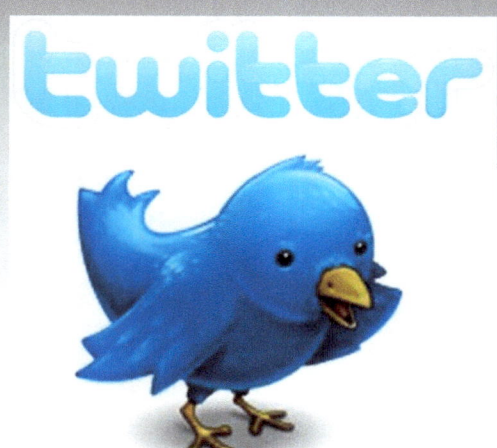

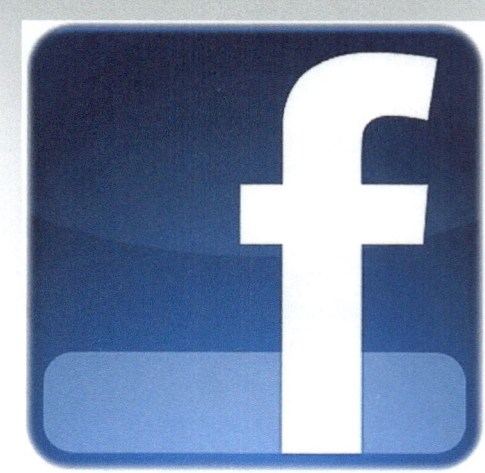

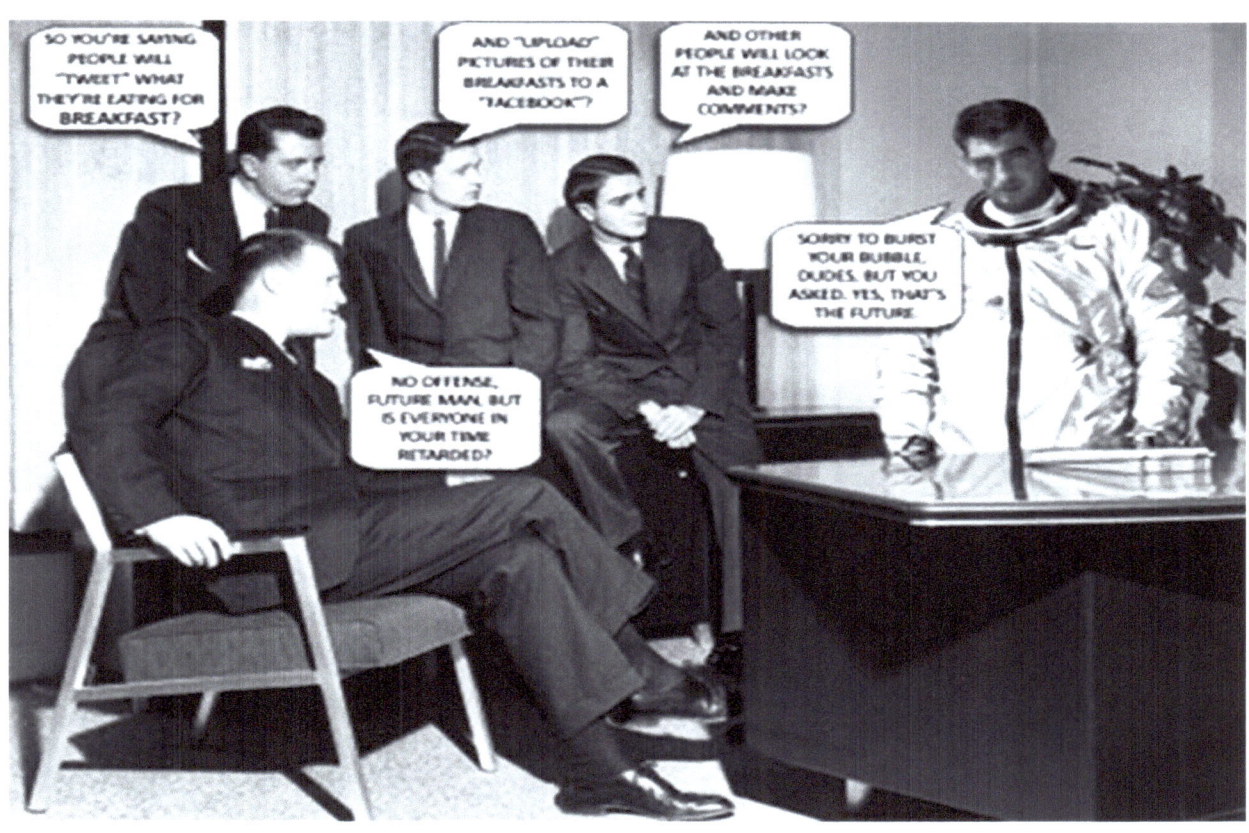

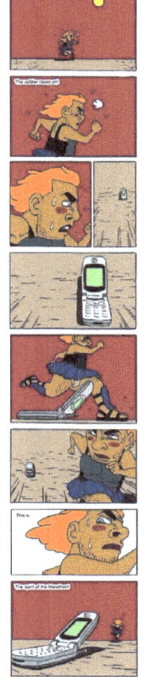

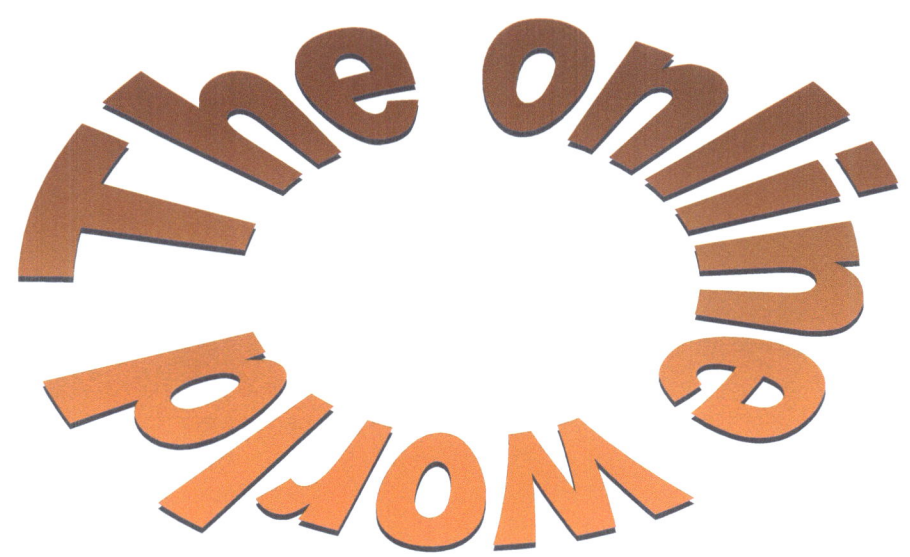

Business Watch: What We Need To Know

Israel approves extension of cease-fire in Gaza; Hamas considers options
Israel late Saturday authorized an extension of the humanitarian cease-fire in Gaza for another 24 hours at the request of the United Nations, Israeli officials told CNN.
Hamas spokesman Osama Hamdan told CNN that the group was still undecided on whether to agree to the truce.

Carjackers run over, kill 3 'sweet' siblings in Philadelphia
Three children helping their mother operate a fruit stand were killed when a stolen SUV plowed into a small crowd on a Philadelphia street corner.
Police Lt. John Stanford said 10-year-old Thomas Reed was pronounced dead on the scene Friday, while 7-year-old Terrence Moore and 15-year-old Keiearra Williams were pronounced dead at the hospital.

Math nerds are taking over Wall Street
Elie Galam is one of them.
Every day, the 30-year old runs 35,000 different trading strategies through software he designed to find a handful of trading ideas with a high statistical probability of making him money.
"It's like seismic imaging," said the Parisian-born Galam, comparing his investing approach to the process used to find pockets of oil.

Rice 'punishment': What is NFL thinking?
My dad told me real men don't hit women.
He believed that because men were physically stronger and mentally tougher, men had the obligation to shield women from harm.
I didn't buy the mentally tougher part, but I did embrace the idea that men were born with a kind of wonderful genetic code that made it impossible for them to pummel any woman, least of all a woman they cherished.

Francona: Putin's real end game in Ukraine
CNN Pentagon Correspondent Barbara Starr reported Thursday that the U.S. intelligence community has information that Russian artillery is firing into eastern Ukraine. The artillery pieces shown in the released footage are Russian M-46 130mm field guns with a range of a little over 16 miles.
Why would the Russians do this? Simple -- this fits into their plan to support pro-Russian separatists in eastern Ukraine. The end game? I believe it is the eventual absorption of that region into the Russian Federation.

Survive The Realestate Market

Chinese homebuyers are flocking to the states…….

More than half of the $22 billion Chinese buyers spent on U.S. homes during the 12 months ended in March was spent in California, Washington and New York, according to the National Association of Realtors.

The hottest markets: Los Angeles, San Francisco, San Diego, New York and Seattle, according to Juwai.com, a Hong Kong-based website that connects Chinese buyers with U.S. properties. So if you are going to buy in the U.S. then look no further. With that much money spent from the Chinese alone we are happy to see the real estate market on the rise.

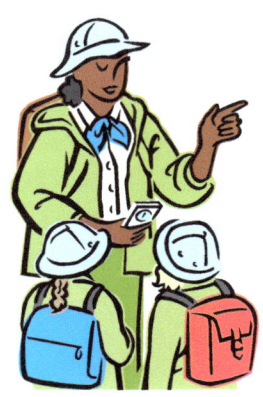

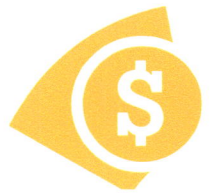

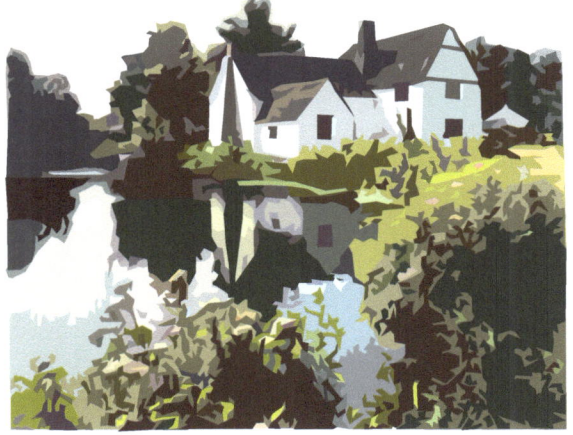

Politics: Special Feature

False Sleep

Here's a roundup of five medical studies published this week that might give you new insights into your health, mind and body. Remember, correlation is not causation -- so if a study finds a connection between two things, it doesn't mean that one causes the other.
Sleep deprivation may lead to false memories
Journal: Psychological Science
Researchers from the University of California say those who are sleep-deprived are more likely to remember false details than those who are not.

Their study was conducted with 104 college-age participants who were split into four groups. Two groups were asked to look at photos of a crime scene upon their arrival, while the other two groups saw the photos the following morning. Half of them went to sleep, while half of them were asked to stay up all night. All were tested on the details of the photographs the following morning.

MH17 crash: Investigators must have full access, Malaysian PM says

More than a week after Malaysia Airlines Flight 17 went down in eastern Ukraine, Malaysian investigators have not yet been able to access the entire crash site, Malaysian Prime Minister Najib Razak said Saturday.
He urged both the pro-Russia rebels and Ukraine's armed forces to cooperate so investigators can access the site fully.
All 298 people aboard the plane died when it crashed on July 17. Of that number, 43 were Malaysian, including 15 crew and two infants, according to Malaysia Airlines.
Nine days later, some human remains still lie scattered amid the debris.

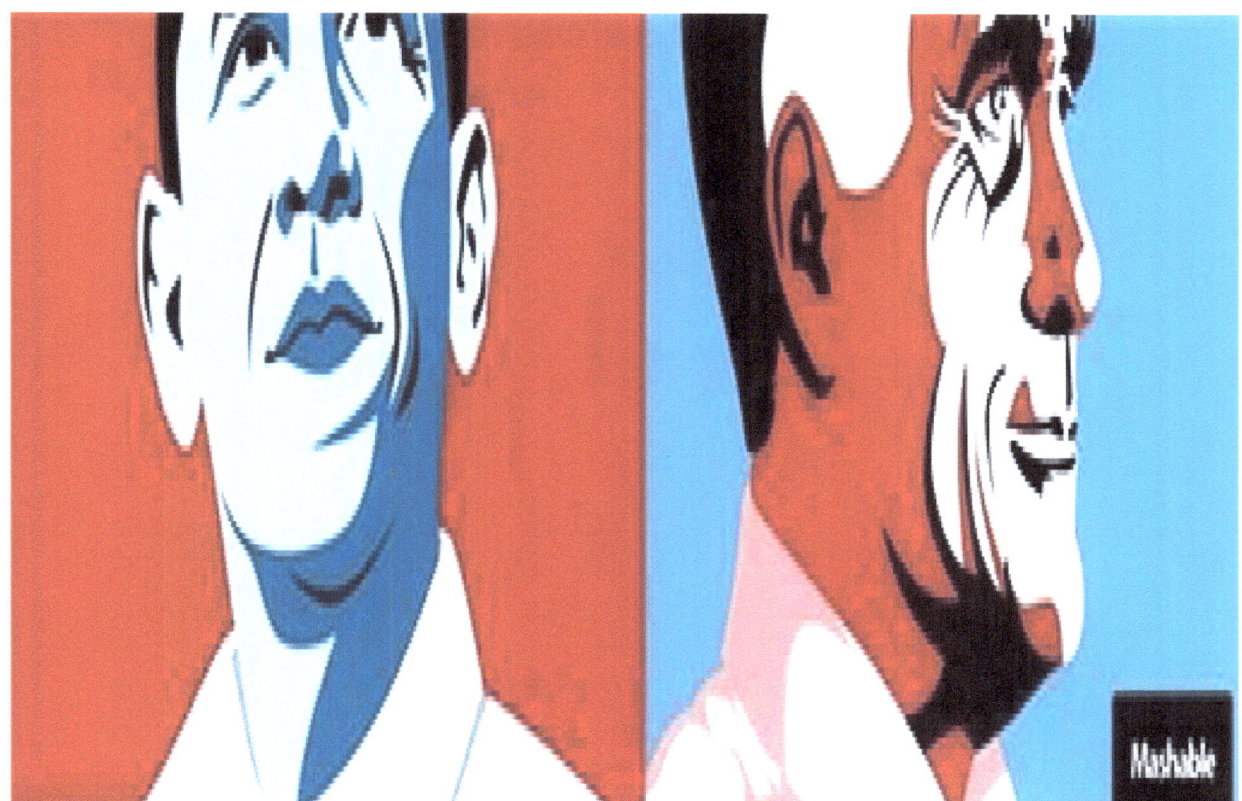

Politics Transformed

THE HIGH-TECH BATTLE FOR YOUR VOTE

August 2014

Sunday	Monday	Tuesday	Wednesday	Thursday	Friday	Saturday
					1	2
3	4	5	6	7	8	9
10	11	12	13	14	15	16
17	18	19	20	21	22	23
24	25	26	27	28	29	30
31						

This month will be a great month!
August will fall on us!

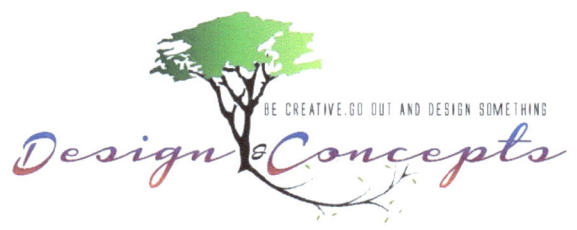

BE CREATIVE.GO OUT AND DESIGN SOMETHING

Join our mailing list and get a free 1 month Subscription to our magazine! www.lisabethdesignmagazine.com

Owner

Design & Concepts L.L.C
Elizabeth Chavez
602-785-1108

Creativedesignconcepts@rocketmail.com

Place orders by email or contact

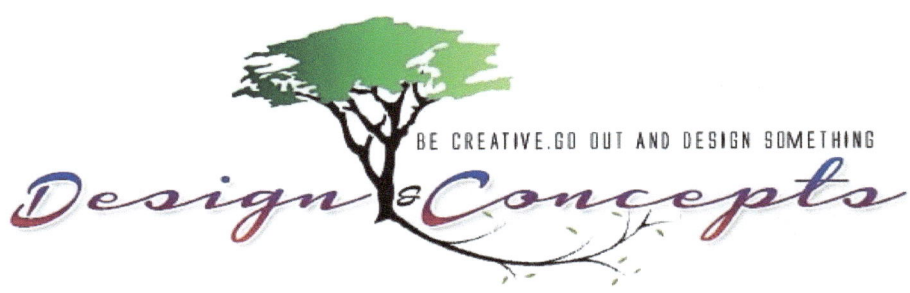

BE CREATIVE.GO OUT AND DESIGN SOMETHING

House of Lisabeths Design Magazine
We were started in 2013 as an independent magazine. Our focus is fashion, health and business. We pride ourselves in the design and diversity we offer.
Exclusivity
Our focus is fashion , health and business. Our fashion section includes tips and trends from all over! We also have a online blog that gets tons of clicks per day, check us out online at ......
Our business section is used for local or national business to place a Ad or listing of them selfs. We have total exclusivity In that they connect with not only our magazine but all of our networks simultaneously.
Our hope is to reach across the world along with Water 4 Kids International.
We plan to donate proceeds to this foundation. Our hope is to provide safe water for east Africa.
Check us out on line, Facebook, Twitter, Tumblr, Amazon, and our affiliates websites like Design & Concepts.

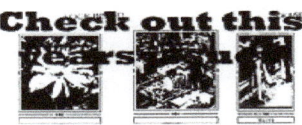

Subscription Information Send To:

Name:

_____

Address:
_____
_____

City, State, Zip:
_____
_____

Credit Card Info: ☐
 Visa ☐
MasterCard ☐
AMEX

Card Number:

_____

Expiration Date:

_____

3 number code:

_____

" Fill out above info and return to address given"
MIAMI
Liz Chavez
8369 NW 66 ST #3684
Miami, FL 33166

Also with your subscription get a free Lisabeth Design T-Shirt

Available for Men and Women

Check out Design & Concepts Blog

Taking new ideas and turning them into key effective and business working matron for your enterprise then most likely that's what your doing now.

As far as media vs print you can see how much of a low cost each has. Similar in certain online groups were we can upload and advertise for free. Key word is always good when working these types of groups you have to remember key words. Lots of web pages will give you the minimu that's were we go in and really find specifics of what it is you do.

To be clear..........

Jane the executive director for Gumbi Gum is wanting to place a new product and have it be presented and marketed to fit a certain time frame.

Next we aske well how is the company receptive to alternative media vs the norm?

There intrigued.....

It's easy to see that by simply tacking the newer ideas and combing capability and interaction we can overcome many demanding questions.

Traditional key words and phrases are always used, used

Join the Cause!
Check out the " Design for Sick Kids Campaign"

Our Mission
In the beginning we wanted a way to show our passion for design.
But this project is turning to be more then that. With so many sick
kids and so much that we can give we thought about giving the gift
of design.

What We Need & What You Get
Here is what we need
1000 cards , either designed by you or who ever
A contribution as well to our campaign

The Impact
With every card made we will donate a dollar and that card to a local
hospital of our choice. So think about all the kids you can help by
creating there Christmas card or birthday card and also the contri-
butions that come with it.
Remember every card made we donate $ 1.00 to the cause
Also share your design with the people and get your picture taken
with the kids

Other Ways You Can Help Check out our websites
www.designandconcepts.net for more updates on more causes!

http://www.indiegogo.com/projects/design-a-card-for-your-kids/

Also with your subscription get a free Lisabeth Design T- Shirt

Available for Men and Women

Design & Concepts Services

Www.Designandconcepts.net
Www.lisabethdesignmagazine.com

Design & Concepts is an online service provider for design and advertising. We specialize in brochures logos and business cards as well as t shirts and stickies. We also do local advertising with in the community. Our prices vary with design but...

Our packages start at $55.00 per package!
Package includes : 200 prints
Gloss or matt finish is $10.00 per set/ per 200

Our Packages also include our Marketing Services, and Discounts on our Advertising Specials in our magazine, House of Lisabeth De-

Also with your subscription get a free Lisabeth Design T- Shirt

Available for Men and Women

Design & Concepts Services:

Create various ads and place it on all social networks, web pages and create you tube videos to sell, demonstrate and promote your product

Also place your ad on any media source that is available
We can take your campaign and place it on any other media resources you have available not just create a web presence awareness but really hit the market.

We use digital media like

Email marketing, social network campaigns, print distribution, custom Web Design and SEO

Funny Definition of the month

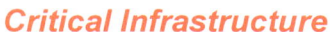
Critical Infrastructure

Critical infrastructure is a term used by governments to describe assets that are essential for the functioning of a society and economy. Most commonly associated with the term are facilities for:

European Union
The European Programme for Critical Infrastructure Protection ([EPCIP]) has been laid out in EU Directives by the Commission (e.g., EU COM(2006) 786 final). It has proposed a list of European critical infrastructures based upon inputs by its Member States.

The German critical-infrastructure protection programme is coordinated by the Federal Ministry of the Interior. Some of its special agencies like the German Federal Office for Information Security or the Federal Office of Civil Protection and Disaster Assistance BBK deliver the respective content, e.g., about IT systems

Recipe Of The Month

Turkey Sausage Tacos

Ingredients
2 tablespoons extra-virgin olive oil
1 carrot, grated
3 scallions, chopped (white and green parts separated)
1 to 2 teaspoons ancho chile powder, plus more for sprinkling
1 pint cherry tomatoes, quartered
1 1/4 pounds turkey sausage, casings removed
12 hard taco shells
1 mango, cubed
Juice of 1 lime
1/4 head romaine lettuce, shredded
1 cup shredded cheddar cheese (about 4 ounces)

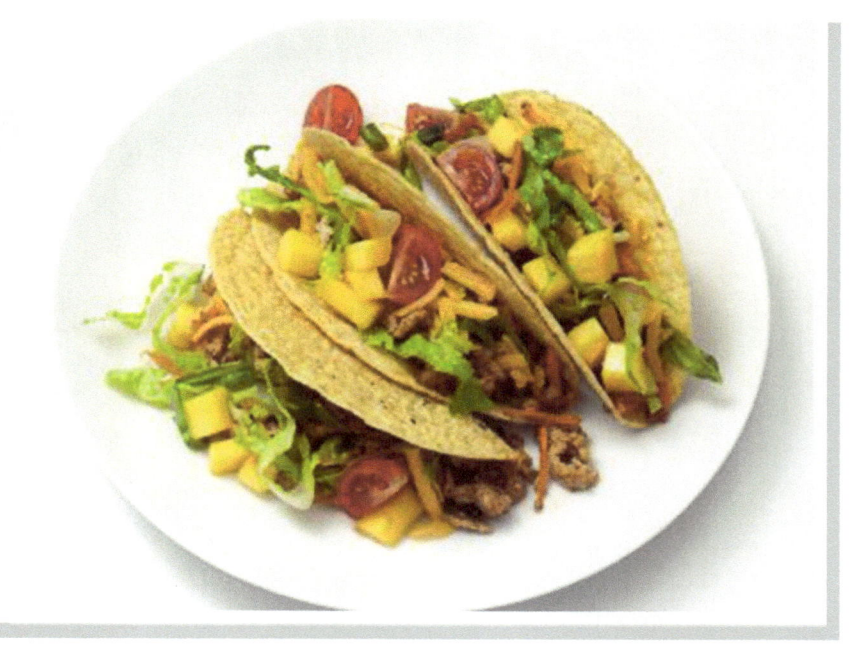

Directions

Preheat the oven to 325 degrees F. Heat the olive oil in a large skillet over medium-high heat. Add the carrot, scallion whites, chile powder and half of the tomatoes. Cook until the tomatoes release their juices, about 3 minutes. Add the sausage and cook, breaking up the meat, until it begins to brown, about 5 minutes. Add half of the scallion greens and cook until most of the liquid has evaporated, about 5 minutes.

Meanwhile, put the taco shells on a baking sheet and warm in the oven, about 6 minutes. Mix the mango with the lime juice in a medium bowl; sprinkle with chile powder. Add the remaining tomatoes and the scallion greens and toss.

Fill the taco shells with the sausage mixture and top with the lettuce, cheese and mango salsa.

ENJOY!!!!!!!!!!

Looking for classifieds, if interested submit your business and information and well help you out!

Liz:
 creativedesignconcepts@rocketmail.com

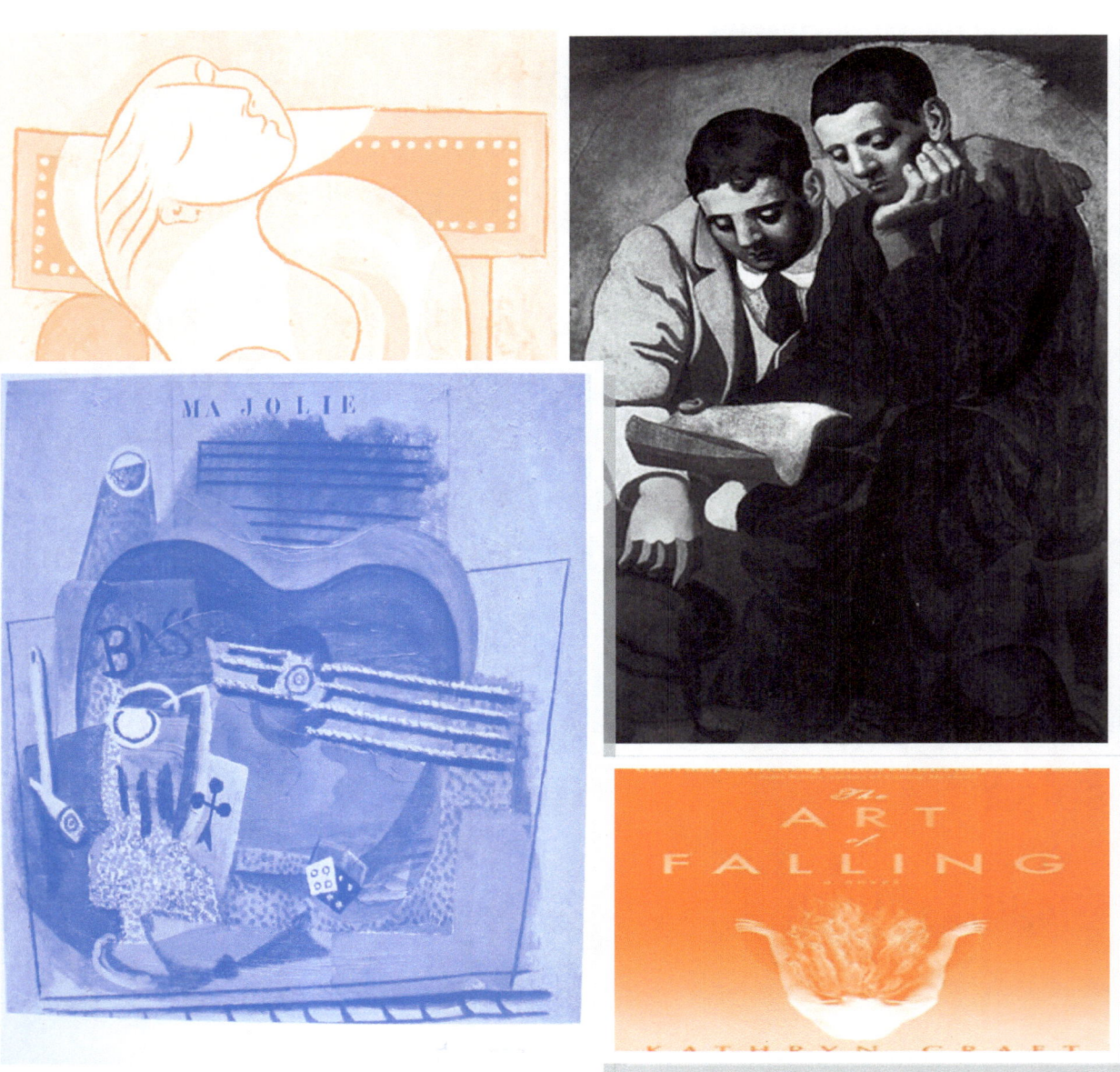

Meet The Editor and Owner…….

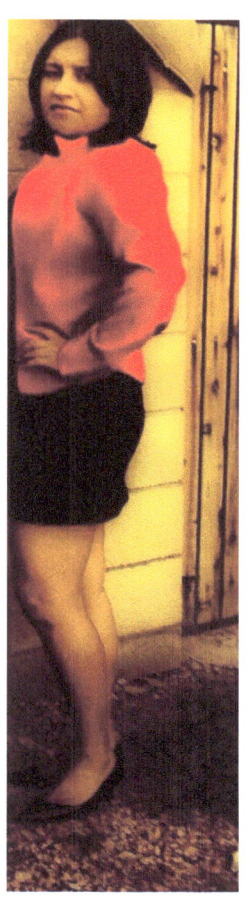 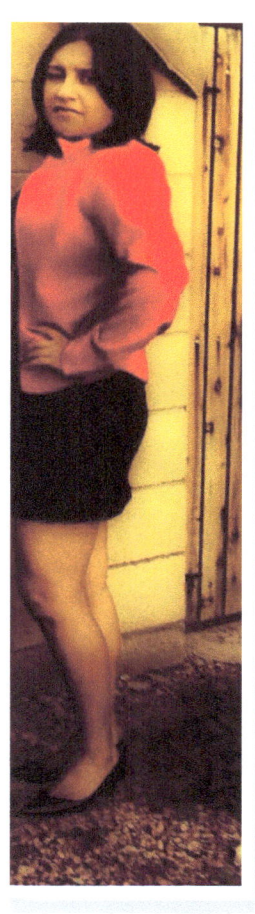 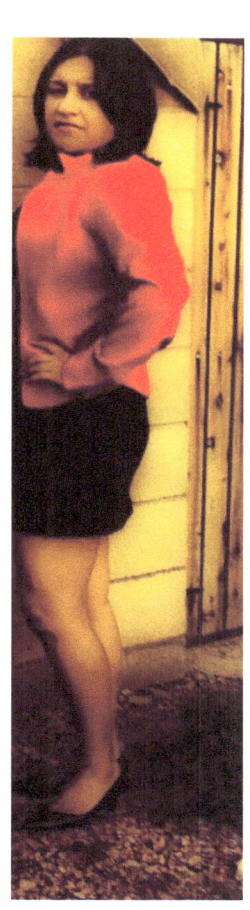

Elizabeth Chavez 27, currently the owner of Design & Concepts LLC , and editor of House of Lisabeth Design Magazine. As an entrepreneur in her own field she manages both her business and love of designing in her everyday life. She works hard by involving all things that she can in many projects that she is involved with. One of her favorite is the Design For Kids Campaign, for her this is not only about kids but about love of the community.

Classifieds

Wells Fargo
Bilingual Insurance call center agent

Take your sales career to a new level at Wells Fargo Insurance. Wells Fargo Insurance is currently seeking Inbound Sales Agents to join our Insurance Call Center team in North Phoenix. solutions to Wells Fargo customers. Our team members describe our work environment as growing, exciting, competitive, and FUN

Store Manager (Retail Financial Services)

As a Store Manager, you will supervise and coordinate the activities of the team members; ensuring adherence to quality standards, deadlines and proper procedures.

Experienced Store Managers, if you are looking for an opportunity to work with an organization where you can grow your retail management career and get rewarded for your efforts, then we have an opportunity for you!

Www.checksmart.com/careers

Molecular Science Liaison

MSL / Research Scientists are responsible for communicating the value of Caris Molecular Intelligence (CMI) to external clients, such as physicians, scientists and other interested parties. This communication primarily involves the preparation of manuscripts for submission to peer-reviewed journals and presentations to customers.
To apply: copy/paste

http://www.careerbuilder.com/jobseeker/
applyonline/applybegin.aspx?
Job_DID=JHR2DT705TDB8MSDR1C&sc_cm
p1=JS_JDP_ApplyNowTop&IPath=QHTV0EJ
7

Lab Technician

Responsible for sampling raw materials.
Responsible for collection of processed water for testing.
Sample production batches
Log in materials as needed
Box finished goods for retain management
Restock supplies
Cross training in other departments
Understand of GMP requirements in the lab
Cleaning of the lab

Www.medix.com

Communication and Marketing Manager

Communication & Marketing Manager is responsible for planning, development and implementation of all AZ Team marketing communications, marketing strategies and public relations activities on behalf of their clients. This job involves one on one sales interaction with customers.

Apply:

Www.azteam.com

Retirement Plan Administrator

We are seeking an experience Retirement Plan Administrator for our office in Phoenix, AZ. In this position, you will be responsible for managing various aspects of plan administration for an assigned case load of clients.

Apply– copy/paste

http://www.careerbuilder.com/jobseeker/applyonline/applybegin.aspx?Job_DID=JHN87H5WQ7PPSZZ244T&sc_cmp1=JS_JDP_ApplyNowTop&IPath=QHTV0YJ7

Customer Service Sales Representative– Inbound Sales

The focus of this position is working with and through others. This person will build and maintain relationships while working closely and accurately within the established guidelines of the position. Our ideal candidate is an effective communicator; someone who is able to stimulate, motivate and engage our customers while being aware of and responsive to their needs and concerns. This person must be friendly, professional and genuinely interested in the needs of our customers while maintaining a positive and proactive approach to the position's established guidelines and goals

Apply : copy/paste
http://www.careerbuilder.com/jobseeker/applyonline/applybegin.aspx?Job_DID=J3J72H64LLYGQ9YLZ60&sc_cmp1=JS_JobDetails_ApplyNow&IPath=QHTV0X

www.ingramcontent.com/pod-product-compliance
Lightning Source LLC
Chambersburg PA
CBHW050355180526
45159CB00005B/2033

* 9 7 8 1 5 0 0 6 5 8 7 5 5 *